COMPREHENSION SKILLS

FACTS

LEVEL C

D1606724

Linda Ward Beech

Tara McCarthy

Donna Townsend

STECK-VAUGHN
ELEMENTARY · SECONDARY · ADULT · LIBRARY
A Harcourt Company

www.steck-vaughn.com

Editorial Director:	Diane Schnell
Project Editor:	Anne Souby
Associate Director of Design:	Cynthia Ellis
Design Manager:	Cynthia Hannon
Media Researcher:	Christina Berry
Production:	Rusty Kay
Cover Illustration:	Stephanie Carter
Cover Production:	Alan Klemp
Photograph:	©iSwoop/FPG International

ISBN 0-7398-2635-2

6 7 8 9 0   BNG   04 03

Facts are things like names, dates, and places. In this book you will practice finding facts.

Facts are all around you. What facts do you see in the picture on this page? What kinds of plants do you see? Is it hot or cold here? The answers to these questions are facts. What other facts can you find in the picture?

What Are Facts?

Facts are sometimes called details. They are small bits of information. Facts are in true stories, such as those in the newspaper. There are facts in stories that people make up, too.

How to Read for Facts

You can find facts by asking yourself questions. Ask *who*, and your answer will be a fact about a person. Ask *what*, and your answer will be a fact about a thing. Ask *where*, and your answer will be a fact about a place. Ask *when*, and your answer will be a fact about a time. Ask *how many* or *how much*, and your answer will be a fact about a number or an amount.

Try It!

Read this story and look for facts as you read. Ask yourself *what* and *where*.

Coober Pedy

Opals are stones that sparkle with many colors. Some of the most beautiful opals come from a town in South Australia. This town is called Coober Pedy. Opals were first found there in 1915. Tourists like to visit this town. They come to buy opals and to see the unusual buildings. Coober Pedy gets very hot in the summer. So most people build their homes underground. In this way the homes stay cool in the summer and warm in the winter. Tourists can stay in an underground hotel.

Did you find these facts when you read the story? Write the facts on the lines below.

◆ What are opals?

Fact: _____

◆ Where is Coober Pedy?

Fact: _____

To check your answers, turn to page 60.

Practice Finding Facts

Below are some practice questions. The first two are already answered. You can do the third one on your own.

_____ **B** **1.** When were opals first found at Coober Pedy?
      A. in 1991   **C.** in summer
      B. in 1915   **D.** in winter

Look at the question and answers again. The word *when* is asking for a time. Reread the story and look for times. Find the sentence that says, "Opals were first found there in 1915." So the correct answer is **B**.

_____ **C** **2.** Tourists like to visit Coober Pedy
      A. to swim   **C.** to buy opals
      B. to dig   **D.** to learn to cook

Look at the question. It has the words *tourists like to visit*. Look for these words in the story. You will find this sentence: "Tourists like to visit this town." Read the next sentence. It says, "They come to buy opals and to see the unusual buildings." The correct answer is **C**.

Now it's your turn to practice. Answer the next question. Write the letter of the correct answer on the line.

_____ **3.** Where can tourists stay?
      A. in a camp   **C.** in an apartment
      B. in a house   **D.** in an underground hotel

To check your answer, turn to page 60.

Using What You Know

Read the following question words and facts that answer the questions. Ask yourself the questions. Then write facts about yourself on the lines.

Who?

Amelia Earhart was a famous pilot.

Geronimo was an Apache chief.

◆ My name is _____.

What?

Seals can't move well on land.

Earthquakes sometimes cause fires.

◆ My favorite animal is the _____.

Where?

Nome is in Alaska.

Mexico is south of Canada.

◆ I live in the city of _____.

When?

Band practice starts at 3:00.

The pool will open on the first of June.

◆ I was born on _____.

How Many?/How Much?

A ton is two thousand pounds.

There were three hundred people in the crowd.

◆ There are _____ students in my class.

Steck-Vaughn • Comprehension Skills Series

How to Use This Book

In this book you will read 25 stories. Each story has two parts. Read the first part. Answer five questions about it. Then read the second part. Answer the next five questions.

You can check your answers by looking at pages 61 and 62. Write the number of correct answers in the score box at the top of the unit page.

Remember

This book asks questions about facts in stories. When you answer the questions, use the facts in the story. You may already know some facts about the subject. But the story will have the answers you need for the questions.

Hints for Better Reading

♦ Look for facts while you are reading the stories. Notice the names of people, animals, and things. Look for places, dates, and times.

♦ Read each question carefully. Think about the facts you need to answer the question. Try to find a sentence in the story that has some of the same words as the question.

♦ Try to remember the facts. If you can't, look back at the story.

Challenge Yourself

Read each story. Cover the story with a sheet of paper. Try to remember the facts. Answer the questions without looking back at the story.

Writing

On pages 30 and 58, there are stories with questions. These do not have answers for you to choose. Think of an answer. Write it in your own words. On pages 31 and 59, you are asked to write your own story. You are given a prewriting activity to help you. You will find suggested answers on page 60. But your answers may be very different.

An Important Bridge

The George Washington Bridge opened in 1931. It joins New York and New Jersey. The bridge changed both states in major ways.

Before the bridge was built, people crossed the Hudson River by boat. The trip was slow. Only a few thousand people crossed the river each day.

The new bridge had eight lanes. Workers in New Jersey could now drive to jobs in New York. New factories opened in New Jersey, too. More New Yorkers found work in New Jersey. New towns sprang up in both states.

_____ **1.** The George Washington Bridge opened
- **A.** in 1913
- **B.** in 1951
- **C.** in 1960
- **D.** in 1931

_____ **2.** The bridge joins New York and
- **A.** Connecticut
- **B.** New Jersey
- **C.** Pennsylvania
- **D.** Canada

_____ **3.** Before the bridge opened, people crossed the Hudson River
- **A.** by foot
- **B.** by car
- **C.** by boat
- **D.** by plane

_____ **4.** The new bridge had
- **A.** six lanes
- **B.** ten lanes
- **C.** four lanes
- **D.** eight lanes

_____ **5.** The bridge caused new towns to spring up in
- **A.** Washington
- **B.** both states
- **C.** New York only
- **D.** New Jersey only

In 1932 about 5 million cars crossed the bridge. By 1960 the number was about 50 million. Soon a second level of the bridge was opened. It added six more lanes for cars. In 2000 about 90 million cars crossed the bridge.

Hundreds of people work on the bridge. Some take money at tollbooths. Others tow away cars that break down on the bridge. Still others patrol the bridge for safety.

The George Washington Bridge is very important. It changed the way of life for people in two states. It helped create new towns and new jobs.

_____ **6.** A total of about 50 million cars crossed the bridge in
      A. 1931   **C.** 1960
      B. 1932   **D.** 2000

_____ **7.** A second level of the bridge added
      A. six lanes   **C.** ten lanes
      B. eight lanes   **D.** fourteen lanes

_____ **8.** In 2000 the bridge was crossed by about
      A. 5 million cars   **C.** 90 million cars
      B. 50 million cars   **D.** 60 million cars

_____ **9.** The number of bridge workers is
      A. hundreds   **C.** one hundred
      B. dozens   **D.** thousands

_____ **10.** Money is collected from drivers
      A. by mail   **C.** at tollbooths
      B. by telephone   **D.** by computer

UNIT 2

Secret Sharks

Most people think of sharks as the ones they see in the movies. These "movie stars" are usually the great white sharks. However, the great whites are just one of 350 kinds of sharks. There are some sharks that have never been seen alive. They live deep in the ocean. They are like the sharks that lived three hundred million years ago.

One example is the goblin shark. It lives hundreds of feet under the sea. Scientists do not believe that it could live if it came to the ocean surface. People in Japan have built a small submarine to learn more about goblin sharks.

Another unusual shark is the megamouth. *Mega* means large and strong. One megamouth that scientists have seen was fifteen feet long. Its mouth was four feet long.

_____ **1.** The sharks usually seen in movies are
  A. gray sharks   **C.** megamouth sharks
  B. goblin sharks   **D.** great white sharks

_____ **2.** How many kinds of sharks are there?
  A. 300   **C.** 4,500
  B. 15   **D.** 350

_____ **3.** The goblin shark will be studied using a
  A. submarine   **C.** library
  B. telescope   **D.** museum

_____ **4.** *Mega* means large and
  A. mean   **C.** strong
  B. rare   **D.** hungry

_____ **5.** The mouth of one megamouth was about
  A. three feet long   **C.** fifteen feet long
  B. four feet long   **D.** sixty feet long

Scientists are trying to learn more about other unusual sharks. One is the frilled shark. This creature has a body like an eel. It has frills on its neck. Scientists want to know what the frilled shark eats. They think it may eat squid.

There are many amazing kinds of small sharks, too. The cookie-cutter shark is only sixteen inches long, but it has very large teeth. This shark also has strong lips. It holds a larger fish with its lips while it scoops out big bites.

Many small sharks hunt together. This way they can kill fish much larger than themselves. One kind of shark that does this is the cigar shark. You can probably guess how this shark got its name. It is the size and shape of a cigar. It is even small enough for you to hold in your hand!

_____ **6.** Scientists are studying
    A. large sharks   **C.** unusual sharks
    B. unkind sharks   **D.** common sharks

_____ **7.** The shark that looks like an eel is the
    A. cigar shark   **C.** eel shark
    B. goblin shark   **D.** frilled shark

_____ **8.** The cookie-cutter shark is
    A. little   **C.** tasty
    B. huge   **D.** fishy

_____ **9.** The cookie-cutter shark has strong
    A. cookies   **C.** eyes
    B. fins   **D.** lips

_____ **10.** One shark that hunts in groups is the
    A. goblin shark   **C.** frilled shark
    B. cigar shark   **D.** ghost shark

UNIT 3

The Story of Rubber

Rubber was brought from South America by travelers. At first people in Europe knew just one way to use it. They would use balls of rubber to rub out pencil marks on paper. That's how rubber got its name!

In those days rubber was shipped in pieces shaped like bottles. First the workers made cuts in the rubber trees. Then they caught the liquid rubber in glass bottles. Soon the liquid became hard. Then the workers broke the bottles. But the hard rubber stayed in the shape of the bottle.

_____ **1.** Rubber came from
    A. New York   **C.** South America
    B. China   **D.** North Carolina

_____ **2.** Rubber got its name because it was used
    A. like a bottle   **C.** to mark on paper
    B. for trees   **D.** to rub out pencil marks

_____ **3.** Rubber was shipped in
    A. glass bottles   **C.** tiny rubber blocks
    B. ball shapes   **D.** pieces shaped like bottles

_____ **4.** The workers
    A. cut down trees   **C.** made cuts in trees
    B. shipped trees   **D.** drank liquid rubber

_____ **5.** The liquid rubber
    A. became soft   **C.** turned brown
    B. tasted good   **D.** became hard

Steck-Vaughn • Comprehension Skills Series

A man had some good ideas about how to use rubber. His name was Charles Macintosh. He found a way to melt hard rubber back into liquid rubber. He would pour the liquid rubber onto cloth. Then he would spread the liquid rubber very thin and cover it with another piece of cloth. Then he let it dry. This rubber cloth did not let water pass through it. Macintosh named this cloth after himself. Soon many people began using macintosh cloth. They used it to make raincoats and mud boots.

Rubber became very important. People poured the liquid rubber into new shapes. Then it became hard again. In this way people made things like water hoses and bicycle tires. They even made parts of machines. In just twenty years rubber changed everyone's life.

_____ **6.** Macintosh had good ideas about how to
    A. use rubber   **C.** make an umbrella
    B. make bottles   **D.** drink rubber

_____ **7.** Macintosh found a way to
    A. water lawns   **C.** melt hard rubber
    B. make glass   **D.** sell bicycles

_____ **8.** Macintosh cloth was used to make
    A. bottles   **C.** machine parts
    B. raincoats   **D.** bedsheets

_____ **9.** People used rubber to make
    A. books   **C.** pillows
    B. pencils   **D.** water hoses

_____ **10.** Rubber changed everyone's life in just
    A. twenty years   **C.** sixty days
    B. forty years   **D.** twelve months

A Running Hero

Jesse Owens was born in Alabama. His real name was James Cleveland Owens. The nickname "Jesse" came from his initials, J.C.

As a child Owens liked to run. He was quite fast. In college he was on the track team. He won many races. In one track meet, he broke three world records and tied a fourth. He did it all in less than one hour!

But his greatest moment came after college. It was the Summer Olympic Games of 1936. The games were held in Germany. Adolf Hitler ruled Germany. Hitler believed Germans were the best athletes. He wanted the world to think this, too.

_____ **1.** Jesse's nickname came from his
   A. father   **C.** grandmother
   B. initials   **D.** teacher

_____ **2.** As a child Owens liked to
   A. hike   **C.** run
   B. ski   **D.** swim

_____ **3.** At a college track meet, Owens broke
   A. 1 world record   **C.** 3 world records
   B. 2 world records **D.** 4 world records

_____ **4.** Owens's greatest moment was in the Olympics of
   A. 1913   **C.** 1936
   B. 1963   **D.** 1923

_____ **5.** Hitler believed that Germans were the best
   A. doctors   **C.** students
   B. athletes   **D.** lawyers

At the Olympics, Owens won four gold medals. He set two Olympic records, too. He made all of America's teams feel proud. The whole world cheered him. Owens was African American. He proved that Hitler's ideas were wrong. He showed that talent has nothing to do with your color or your background.

Owens felt that sports could help solve racial problems. He spent much of his life helping others. He worked mainly with youth. He traveled a great deal and gave many speeches. He talked about fair play and love of one's country. He was a hero to people all around the world.

_____ **6.** In the Summer Olympics, Owens won four
  A. silver medals   **C.** bronze medals
  B. gold medals   **D.** copper medals

_____ **7.** Owens set a total of two
  A. German records   **C.** American records
  B. world records   **D.** Olympic records

_____ **8.** Owens proved that
  A. skill is luck   **C.** running is bad
  B. Hitler was right   **D.** Hitler was wrong

_____ **9.** Owens believed that sports could help end
  A. back problems   **C.** racial troubles
  B. poor diets   **D.** money problems

_____**10.** Owens worked mostly with
  A. youngsters   **C.** African Americans
  B. senior citizens   **D.** Germans

The Sound Machine's Deaf Inventor

Thomas Edison was one of the greatest inventors of all time. One of his best-known works was the phonograph. He built it in 1877. It was the first machine to record and play sound. Any inventor of this sound machine could be called great. But for Edison, it was a very great deed. That's because he was partly deaf.

When Tom was a teen, he worked on a train. One day he was late for work. He ran for the train just as it was pulling out of the station. The conductor tried to help the boy. He grabbed Tom by the ears and pulled him up. "I felt something snap inside my head," Edison said later. From that point on, he grew more and more deaf.

_____ **1.** Thomas Edison was a great
   A. doctor   **C.** inventor
   B. writer   **D.** president

_____ **2.** One of Edison's best-known works was the
   A. telephone   **C.** television
   B. phonograph   **D.** photograph

_____ **3.** The phonograph was built in
   A. 1887   **C.** 1877
   B. 1787   **D.** 1777

_____ **4.** Edison was
   A. totally blind **C.** partly blind
   B. totally deaf   **D.** partly deaf

_____ **5.** Tom was hurt when his ears were pulled by a
   A. teacher   **C.** singer
   B. conductor   **D.** bully

Despite his hearing loss, Edison went on to invent many things. His favorite was the phonograph. Edison tested it once it was built. He spoke into the mouth of the machine. He said, "Mary had a little lamb." The machine played back his words.

How could Edison build a sound machine if he was deaf? He had a trick. He pressed his ear up to the machine to feel it vibrate.

Edison could have had an operation so he could hear again. But he chose not to. He said that being deaf helped him. He said it let him think better. Outside noises did not distract him at work. That was another part of his genius!

_____ **6.** The phonograph was Edison's
      A. only invention   **C.** last invention
      B. first invention   **D.** favorite invention

_____ **7.** Edison's phonograph
      A. did not work   **C.** made words louder
      B. helped Mary   **D.** repeated his words

_____ **8.** Edison could hear by pressing his ear to
      A. a paper cup   **C.** a hearing aid
      B. another person   **D.** the phonograph

_____ **9.** Edison did not have an ear operation because he
      A. had no choice   **C.** was afraid
      B. chose not to   **D.** was too busy

_____**10.** Edison said that being deaf
      A. hurt him   **C.** made him tired
      B. annoyed him   **D.** aided him

Beard Beginnings

There's nothing really new about beards. Men have been growing beards for thousands of years. If a man does not shave his chin and the sides of his face, a beard will grow. Long ago all men had beards.

The first men to shave off their beards were the early Egyptians. But not all Egyptian men shaved. Some spent hours caring for their beards. They dyed them, braided them, and even wove gold threads into them. The kings and queens of Egypt sometimes wore false beards called postiches. A postiche was a sign of royalty. It was made of metal and attached to the chin with straps of gold.

Some men in ancient Greece wore beards. They thought a beard was a sign of wisdom. Socrates was a famous Greek who wore a beard. He was also thought to be a wise man.

_____ **1.** If a man doesn't shave, he will grow a
     A. nose   **C.** braid
     B. beard   **D.** chin

_____ **2.** Long ago all men had
     A. postiches   **C.** gold
     B. beards   **D.** wisdom

_____ **3.** The kings of Egypt sometimes wore
     A. false beards   **C.** diamond beards
     B. wise beards   **D.** cloth beards

_____ **4.** A postiche was a sign of
     A. weakness   **C.** royalty
     B. loyalty   **D.** marriage

_____ **5.** A famous Greek who wore a beard was
     A. Postiche   **C.** Egyptian
     B. Burnside   **D.** Socrates

For hundreds of years, beards were not popular. They became fashionable again in the 1500s. One style of beard was called the goatee. This small, pointed beard hangs from the lower lip and chin. It looks like the beard of a goat. In the 1600s another style of beard became popular. It was called the Vandyke. This beard was named after a famous painter of the time, Anthony Vandyke.

Men wore their whiskers in still other ways in the 1800s. Some men wore muttonchops. These are really side whiskers that are shaped like lamp chops. *Mutton* is another word for *lamb*. Another style was named after an American general. His name was Ambrose E. Burnside. Burnside shaved his chin but grew short whiskers on the sides of his face. At first people called these burnsides. Later the name got mixed up and became *sideburns*.

_____ **6.** The goatee became the fashion in the
     A. 1400s   **C.** 1700s
     B. 1500s   **D.** 1800s

_____ **7.** The Vandyke beard was named after a
     A. general   **C.** painter
     B. king   **D.** lamb

_____ **8.** Muttonchops are really
     A. postiches   **C.** chin whiskers
     B. lambs   **D.** side whiskers

_____ **9.** Sideburns were named for an American
     A. officer   **C.** lamb chop
     B. artist   **D.** mutton

_____ **10.** Sideburns were popular in the
     A. 1500s   **C.** 1700s
     B. 1600s   **D.** 1800s

A Woman to Count On

Romana Banuelos was born in Arizona. As a young girl, she moved with her family to Mexico. Romana did well in school. She liked math. She hoped one day to find a job that would let her use her math skills.

When Romana was 24, she took a big chance. She put money into a business. It was a tortilla stand in Los Angeles. Over time the business grew. It became a $5 million food company!

Romana was now rich. But she didn't stop there. Soon she started a new bank. At the time it was the only United States bank run by Mexican Americans. Later she also formed a special fund. It gave Mexican Americans money to go to college.

_____ **1.** Romana Banuelos was born in
    A. Mexico   **C.** New Mexico
    B. Arizona   **D.** Los Angeles

_____ **2.** In school Romana especially liked
    A. reading   **C.** math
    B. spelling   **D.** science

_____ **3.** At age 24 Romana put money into a
    A. bank   **C.** clothing company
    B. college   **D.** tortilla stand

_____ **4.** Her business became worth
    A. $50 million   **C.** $5 billion
    B. $500 million   **D.** $5 million

_____ **5.** Her fund gave Mexican Americans money to
    A. find a job   **C.** get clothing
    B. go to college   **D.** buy a home

Romana worked hard to help people. Her work made her well known. Soon she had a new job. President Nixon asked her to be treasurer of the United States. She held the job for three years. She was the first Mexican American woman to hold this post.

In her job Romana wrote and signed checks from the government. Her name was stamped on all paper bills. Part of her job was to make sure all worn-out bills were destroyed.

Romana's work inspired many people. She was a role model to young Hispanics. Young women admired Romana, too. She became a hero to all America.

_____ **6.** President Nixon asked Romana to serve as United States
     A. vice-president   **C.** treasurer
     B. ambassador   **D.** delegate

_____ **7.** Romana worked under Nixon for
     A. three years   **C.** five years
     B. four years   **D.** six years

_____ **8.** At work Romana wrote and signed government
     A. laws   **C.** contracts
     B. books   **D.** checks

_____ **9.** Her name appeared on all
     A. posters   **C.** paper money
     B. pictures   **D.** coins

_____ **10.** She made sure worn-out bills were
     A. destroyed   **C.** checked
     B. stamped   **D.** signed

Dutch People in New York

New York City was not always a big city. The land that was to become New York was once covered with trees. The Dutch people first came to this pretty land in 1609. The people missed their homes that they had left across the sea. So they made new homes in the green land they found. New York then looked very much like Holland.

Here the Dutch people tried to live in the same ways they had lived in Holland. They worked hard, but they also played many games. One of these games was bowling. Back then people bowled outside on the grass. Today Bowling Green is a grassy park in New York City. It is the place where the Dutch people bowled long ago.

_____ **1.** New York was once covered with
   A. birds   **C.** trees
   B. games   **D.** flowers

_____ **2.** Dutch people came to New York in
   A. 1907   **C.** 1505
   B. 1609   **D.** 1006

_____ **3.** New York looked like
   A. France   **C.** a grassy park
   B. Holland   **D.** it does today

_____ **4.** The Dutch people played
   A. cards   **C.** the piano
   B. ball   **D.** many games

_____ **5.** Bowling Green is a
   A. baseball field   **C.** grassy park
   B. special color   **D.** place in Holland

The Dutch people built their homes next to the sea. They built the walls of stone. The houses had special doors. Someone could open the top part of the door and talk to a friend. But the bottom part of the door could stay closed. The bottom part kept the pigs and chickens out of the house.

New York is very different today. But the Dutch people left us many things that help us remember the past. We can still find many Dutch houses. The Dutch people had firefighters and police officers, just as we do today. The Dutch people even started the first free school in New York.

_____ **6.** The Dutch people lived
      A. by the sea   **C.** on hillsides
      B. in the woods   **D.** near the rocks

_____ **7.** The walls of the houses were made of
      A. stone   **C.** bricks
      B. grass   **D.** wood

_____ **8.** The Dutch door kept out
      A. friends   **C.** pigs and chickens
      B. flies   **D.** birds and crickets

_____ **9.** Signs of the Dutch that remain are their
      A. clothes   **C.** pigs and chickens
      B. houses   **D.** trees

_____ **10.** The Dutch people in New York used
      A. mail carriers   **C.** firefighters
      B. elevators   **D.** school libraries

Pretty Pearls

Down, down go the divers. At the bottom of the sea, they pick up oysters that grow there. The divers bring the oysters up to the surface of the water. Other workers then put the oysters into wire baskets. These baskets hang from floating rafts. The oysters float safely in the baskets in the sea.

When the oysters are three years old, they are removed from the sea. Experts put tiny round beads inside the oysters. Then the oysters are returned in their baskets to the sea. From time to time, workers pull the baskets out of the sea. They clean off moss and seaweed from the oyster shells.

Why do the oysters receive such good care? In a few years, the oyster will cover the bead with a shiny coating. It will then become a pearl.

_____ **1.** An oyster grows at the bottom of the
    A. sea   **C.** pearl
    B. raft   **D.** basket

_____ **2.** Oysters are put into wire baskets that
    A. hang   **C.** sink
    B. swim   **D.** dive

_____ **3.** A bead is put inside the oyster when it is
    A. found   **C.** three years old
    B. cleaned   **D.** two years old

_____ **4.** From time to time, workers
    A. sell oysters   **C.** taste oysters
    B. open oysters   **D.** clean oysters

_____ **5.** The bead inside an oyster becomes a
    A. plant   **C.** ruby
    B. moss   **D.** pearl

Steck-Vaughn • Comprehension Skills Series

The story of pearls goes back to 2206 B.C. That is more than four thousand years ago. At that time people in China gave pearls as gifts or rewards. In Persia pearls were used to decorate clay pots. In many countries people thought of pearls as jewels of love. Husbands gave them to their wives. Kings and queens gave them to one another.

Over the years people have used pearls in many ways. They have decorated crowns and swords with them. They have sewn pearls into fine clothing. Most often people have used pearls in pins, necklaces, rings, and bracelets.

The pearl is the birthstone for people who are born in June. The pearl is said to stand for health, wealth, and a long life. Perhaps that is why many people say that pearls become more beautiful with age.

_____ **6.** Early Chinese people gave pearls as
     A. presents   **C.** kings
     B. baskets   **D.** birthstones

_____ **7.** Long ago in Persia, pearls were used on
     A. walls   **C.** oysters
     B. gifts   **D.** pottery

_____ **8.** People often use pearls in
     A. pottery   **C.** jewelry
     B. flowers   **D.** baskets

_____ **9.** Pearls are birthstones for the month of
     A. April   **C.** July
     B. June   **D.** December

_____ **10.** As pearls age, many people think they are
     A. more costly   **C.** less valuable
     B. less helpful   **D.** more lovely

A Rare Voice

Marian Anderson always loved to sing. As a child she sang in church choirs. After high school she studied voice. Her teacher knew that she had a rare gift. Soon Marian went on concert tours. She traveled all across the United States. She sang in Europe, too. Fans far and near praised her sweet voice.

But Anderson did not have an easy time in her career. She was African American. Some people did not want her to sing because of this. In 1939 a women's group would not let her perform in a hall in Washington, D.C. This caused other people to get angry. One of those people was Eleanor Roosevelt, the President's wife.

_____ **1.** As a child Marian sang in
    A. church choirs   **C.** TV commercials
    B. school clubs   **D.** Broadway shows

_____ **2.** After high school Marian began to go on
    A. album covers   **C.** concert tours
    B. vacations   **D.** television shows

_____ **3.** Some people didn't want her to sing because she
    A. was too loud   **C.** was African American
    B. was too soft   **D.** charged too much

_____ **4.** In 1939 a group kept her from singing in
    A. a school   **C.** the White House
    B. a church   **D.** a hall

_____ **5.** Eleanor Roosevelt got angry because a group wouldn't let Marian
    A. sing in church   **C.** perform in a hall
    B. study voice   **D.** travel in Europe

Mrs. Roosevelt could not get the women's group to change its mind. So she made a new plan. She asked Anderson to sing outdoors. More than 75,000 people came to hear her. She gained more fans as a result.

Anderson won many awards for her singing. She was the first African American to sing solo with New York's main opera company. Fans praised her for her fine work. Some said she had the best opera voice of all time.

In time Anderson stopped singing. But she went on to do more good work. She served as a delegate to the United Nations. She won the U.N. peace prize in 1977.

_____ **6.** After a change in plans, Anderson sang
      A. outside   **C.** at the White House
      B. in a theater   **D.** in a record studio

_____ **7.** Her program was attended by about
      A. 750 people   **C.** 7,500 people
      B. 75,000 people   **D.** 750,000 people

_____ **8.** Anderson sang solo with New York's main
      A. church   **C.** television station
      B. Broadway show   **D.** opera company

_____ **9.** Anderson worked in the United Nations as a
      A. translator   **C.** singer
      B. secretary   **D.** delegate

_____ **10.** Anderson was awarded a peace prize in
      A. 1987   **C.** 1977
      B. 1978   **D.** 1777

Her Honor

The United States Supreme Court is the highest court of the land. For many years only men were Supreme Court justices. That was true until 1981. That year Sandra Day O'Connor became a Supreme Court justice. She was the first woman to do so.

Sandra's first teacher was her mother. Later Sandra went to school. Sandra finished high school when she was just sixteen. Then she followed her dream to study law. She was in law school for five years. When she finished law school, she couldn't find a job. Very few companies wanted women who knew law!

_____ **1.** The highest court of the land is the
    A. World Court   **C.** Supreme Court
    B. State Court   **D.** United States Court

_____ **2.** Only men served on the Supreme Court
    A. after 1990   **C.** until 1981
    B. after 1811   **D.** until 200 years ago

_____ **3.** Sandra's first teacher was her
    A. mother   **C.** sister
    B. father   **D.** grandmother

_____ **4.** Sandra's dream was to
    A. go to school   **C.** stay at home
    B. study law   **D.** work on a ranch

_____ **5.** When Sandra finished law school, she
    A. found a job   **C.** couldn't find a job
    B. got sick   **D.** went back to school

Steck-Vaughn • Comprehension Skills Series

Sandra married a man she met in law school. They both got jobs as lawyers. For a while Sandra had her own law office. Then she and her husband had a son. Sandra decided to stay home. Sandra and her husband had two more sons.

After nine years Sandra became a judge in Arizona. She was a judge there for seven years. Then one of the justices from the Supreme Court left. So the Supreme Court needed another justice. The President of the United States heard about Sandra. He asked her to become a justice on the Supreme Court. She eagerly said, "Yes!"

_____ **6.** Sandra and her husband were both
    A. doctors   **C.** teachers
    B. lawyers   **D.** bankers

_____ **7.** Sandra had
    A. three sons   **C.** a son and a daughter
    B. two daughters   **D.** four children

_____ **8.** Sandra stayed home with her children for
    A. nine years   **C.** twenty years
    B. seven years   **D.** five years

_____ **9.** One of the justices left the
    A. High Court   **C.** Arizona Court
    B. World Court   **D.** Supreme Court

_____ **10.** The President asked Sandra to be a
    A. student   **C.** judge in an Arizona court
    B. lawyer   **D.** justice on the Supreme Court

The Oldest Toy

One of the very first toys was simple and round. It was a ball. The first balls were just rocks that were round and smooth. People liked kicking rocks to see how far the rocks would go. They also threw rocks to see if they could hit certain things with them.

Bowling was first played thousands of years ago in Egypt. A ball made of rock was rolled through a short tunnel. People tried to knock down the nine rock pieces at the other end of the tunnel.

Later bowling was played in Germany. At first people used a stone ball and one wooden pin. Then they used a ball made of wood. The number of pins also changed. Sometimes people used three pins. Other times people used as many as seventeen pins.

_____ **1.** One of the very first toys was
  A. round   **C.** square
  B. sharp   **D.** flat

_____ **2.** People liked kicking rocks to see how
  A. soft they were   **C.** high they would go
  B. hard they were   **D.** far they would go

_____ **3.** The first bowling game was played
  A. in Egypt   **C.** in the United States
  B. in Germany   **D.** with one wooden pin

_____ **4.** A rock ball was rolled through a
  A. field   **C.** tunnel
  B. street   **D.** sidewalk

_____ **5.** At first in Germany people used
  A. three pins   **C.** one wooden pin
  B. seventeen pins   **D.** one hundred pins

Native Americans made up games that used balls. Some of them played a game that was like basketball. They even had a ball made of rubber. They got the rubber from the trees where they lived.

Handball games started in Europe. Children liked to bounce small balls made of animal skin against the sides of buildings. They especially liked the high stone walls of churches. Later people started hitting the ball to each other over a net. At first they used only their hands. But then they began to wrap their hands with string. They also added a stick. The game of tennis started from the game of handball.

_____ **6.** Some Native Americans had a ball that
     A. didn't bounce   **c.** they hit with a bat
     B. fell apart   **D.** was made of rubber

_____ **7.** Rubber comes from
     A. rivers   **c.** animal skins
     B. trees   **D.** the ground

_____ **8.** Handball was first played in
     A. prisons   **c.** Europe
     B. Japan   **D.** churches

_____ **9.** People first hit balls over nets with their
     A. gloves   **c.** hands
     B. feet   **D.** shoes

_____**10.** Tennis came from the game of
     A. handball   **c.** bowling
     B. basketball   **D.** skin ball

Writing

Read the story below. Think about the facts. Then answer the questions in complete sentences.

Have you ever seen a comet? It looks like a fuzzy star with a tail. It travels along a path in the sky. When the comet comes near the sun, its tail looks long and bright.

Long ago most people thought that comets appeared by chance. They did not think they traveled on a set path or time. But Edmond Halley disagreed. He was an English scientist. He claimed that comets came near the sun at set times. Halley mapped the path of one comet. He had seen it in 1682. He predicted it would appear again in 1758. He was right. Today that comet is known as Halley's Comet. It is seen about every 77 years.

1. What does a comet look like?

_____

_____

2. When does a comet's tail look long and bright?

_____

_____

3. How often can Halley's Comet be seen?

_____

_____

To check your answers, turn to page 60.

Steck-Vaughn • Comprehension Skills Series

Prewriting

Think of an idea you might write about, such as a planet or a way to travel in space. Write the idea in the center of the idea web below. Then fill out the rest of the web with facts.

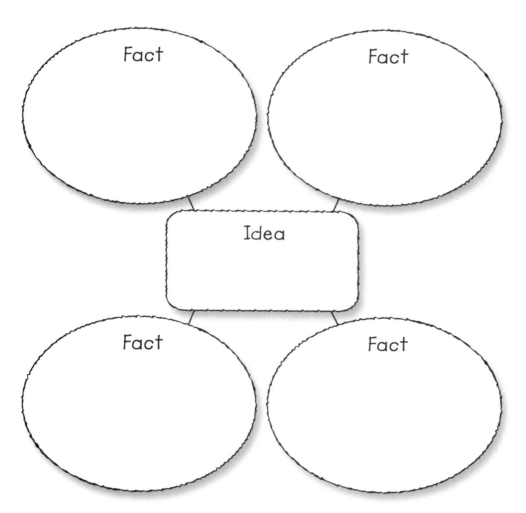

On Your Own

Now use another sheet of paper to write a story about your idea. Use the facts from your idea web.

To check your answers, turn to page 60.

What Is *That* For?

Tools can become extinct, just like animals. When people no longer need the tools, they stop making them. You can find extinct tools in old houses and barns.

In an old house, you might find something shaped like a tall coffee pot. It has a lid, but it doesn't have a bottom or a handle. It sits on a metal saucer. This strange thing is a fly trap. People would put honey or sugar in the saucer. Then they would put the trap on top of the saucer. Flies crawled in to get the sweet bait, but then they could not escape.

Suppose you find a large, deep metal container. It sits low to the ground and has little wheels. You've discovered a sink that moves! After a meal someone would roll the sink into the dining room. People would put their dishes into it. Then the sink was rolled back to the kitchen.

_____ **1.** Old tools can be like
   A. used clothes   **C.** extinct animals
   B. old barns   **D.** strange saucers

_____ **2.** The fly trap was shaped like a
   A. coffee pot   **C.** screen wire
   B. metal plate   **D.** little wheel

_____ **3.** Flies crawled into the trap to get
   A. caught   **C.** the saucers
   B. the honey   **D.** shaken

_____ **4.** The sink could
   A. move   **C.** eat
   B. clean   **D.** walk

_____ **5.** People used the sink to
   A. make dishes   **C.** have fun
   B. serve meals   **D.** clear tables

In an old barn, you might see different kinds of old wooden tools. One is shaped like a big picture frame. Another is shaped like a beehive, but it has a ring at the top and several sticks at the bottom. Both of these things are *pokes*. Farmers hung pokes around the necks of farm animals so the animals could not get through a fence. You might find tiny pokes shaped like the letter *A*. These pokes were put around the necks of geese.

Here's a long, metal T-shaped object. At the bottom there are sharp, curled pieces of iron. This tool is a *sugar devil*. It was used for scraping food from the bottom of a barrel.

Finally, how about all these tiny hammers? They're only about five inches long. They're *Yankee snow knockers*. They were hung on sleds to knock snow from horses' hooves.

_____ **6.** One kind of poke is shaped like
    A. pigs   **C.** a picture frame
    B. hammers   **D.** the letter *B*

_____ **7.** Pokes kept animals from
    A. going inside   **C.** knocking down frames
    B. eating rings   **D.** getting through fences

_____ **8.** The A-shaped poke was for
    A. bees   **C.** geese
    B. horses   **D.** wood

_____ **9.** People used a sugar devil to
    A. curl iron   **C.** make barrels
    B. bake sweets   **D.** scrape food

_____ **10.** Snow knockers were put on
    A. sleds   **C.** hooves
    B. hammers   **D.** doors

U N I T

14

The Most Important Food

Bread might have been the first food that people made. The earliest people pounded nuts and seeds between two rocks to make a kind of flour. The bread made from this flour was flat, heavy, and dry. It probably didn't taste very good. But it was an important food.

Later, people began growing grass seeds themselves. The people called the grasses wheat, rice, and corn. They made flour mills from big, flat rocks. These rocks were very heavy. They had to be turned around and around by horses. Or sometimes the water from a river moved the rocks. The flour improved. So the bread tasted much better, too.

_____ **1.** The earliest people made flour by
  A. eating food   **C.** pounding seeds and nuts
  B. pulling leaves   **D.** catching animals

_____ **2.** At first bread was
  A. brown   **C.** flat, heavy, and dry
  B. delicious   **D.** light and puffy

_____ **3.** People called the grasses
  A. milk and honey   **C.** seeds, nuts, and bread
  B. rocks and water   **D.** wheat, rice, and corn

_____ **4.** The rocks in flour mills were moved by
  A. horses   **C.** machines
  B. cows   **D.** people

_____ **5.** When the flour improved, the bread was
  A. worse   **C.** the same
  B. better   **D.** much harder

Steck-Vaughn • Comprehension Skills Series

People began to find new ways to make bread. They found a way to make the bread puff up with little air bubbles. As time went by, people added new things to bread. They used butter, milk, and even eggs. Sometimes they would put fruit and nuts in it. Some bread became so sweet that we now call it cake. People also tried making different shapes and sizes of bread. They made little round bread that we call rolls. They made very flat bread that we call pancakes.

Today bread has many shapes, sizes, colors, and tastes. It is still a very important food.

_____ **6.** Bread puffed up because it had
    A. eggs   **C.** sugar cubes
    B. milk   **D.** air bubbles

_____ **7.** To make new bread, people added
    A. meat   **C.** vegetables
    B. eggs   **D.** leaves

_____ **8.** We call bread that is little and round
    A. pie   **C.** corn bread
    B. rolls   **D.** cookies

_____ **9.** Pancakes are a kind of bread that is
    A. flat   **C.** very salty
    B. black   **D.** made with nuts

_____ **10.** As a food, bread has changed, but it is still
    A. awful   **C.** sour
    B. salty   **D.** important

Speak to Me, Honey!

A brass robot moves around. A flat wing on its body whirs with a faint buzz. Sugar water drips from a small tube. All at once several bees fly away from the hive where the robot performs. The robot has "talked" to the bees. It has told them where they can find food.

Years ago Nobel Prize winner Karl von Frisch found out that bees dance when they want to "talk" to other bees. Later, experts learned that bees can hear the beating sound of other bees' wings. They now know that bees use these signals to tell other bees where food can be found.

Bees also learn about the flavor of their next meal from their dancing friends. When bees return to a hive, they bring a sample of the meal they have just enjoyed. As they dance, other bees gather around to taste the sample.

_____ 1. The one who learned that bees "talk" was
     A. a bee keeper   **C.** Karl von Frisch
     B. a robot maker   **D.** a brass expert

_____ 2. Later, experts learned that bees can hear
     A. human voices   **C.** other bees' wings
     B. other insects   **D.** classical music

_____ 3. The bees' signals tell other bees where to
     A. find water   **C.** see another bee
     B. find food   **D.** see another hive

_____ 4. When bees return to a hive, they bring
     A. flowers   **C.** new wings
     B. eggs   **D.** a sample of food

_____ 5. As bees dance, other bees in the hive
     A. go to sleep   **C.** go to other hives
     B. die   **D.** gather around

Some people wanted to prove that what von Frisch had said was true. In August of 1988, they made a bee robot. They knew that bees would attack bees from other hives. So they had to make their "bee" smell like the bees in the hive where it would dance. They did this by rubbing wax on the robot and placing it in the hive for one night.

The next day they put the robot in the hive. They guided the brass "bee" with a machine. They slowly led it in a figure eight. Then they made its wing buzz. Other bees began to gather around the robot. The bees "asked" the robot for a taste of their next meal. The robot makers were ready. A drop of sugar water flowed down a tube near the robot's head. The bees tasted the sweet drink. All at once a bee left the hive. Then another followed. The robot makers cheered. They had "talked" to bees.

_____ **6.** Some people made a robot that could
    A. fly   **C.** "speak" to bees
    B. sting   **D.** "see" bees

_____ **7.** The people knew that real bees could
    A. hide the robot   **C.** smell the robot
    B. eat the robot   **D.** color the robot

_____ **8.** The robot bee was made of
    A. wood   **C.** plastic
    B. brass   **D.** paper

_____ **9.** The robot makers moved their bee
    A. into the hive   **C.** under the hive
    B. over the hive   **D.** out of the hive

_____**10.** The robot makers fed the bees
    A. wax   **C.** honey
    B. water   **D.** sugar water

Save the Turkeys!

Turkeys are interesting birds. They don't take off and fly smoothly like other birds. Turkeys take off like helicopters. They go almost straight up and can fly fast. One wild turkey was timed flying at 55 miles per hour.

Turkeys differ from most birds in other ways, too. Male turkeys have snoods and wattles. The snood is a flap of skin above the beak. It can grow to be five inches long. Male turkeys use their snoods to attract females.

A turkey's wattle is the bumpy skin on his neck. It can grow very large. And it can turn from red to white and back again. Some people think that this happens when the turkey wants to send a message. He might be trying to attract a female. Or he might be sending a signal to another male that says, "Stay away!"

_____ **1.** When a turkey takes off, it flies
  A. slowly   **C.** straight up
  B. smoothly   **D.** near the ground

_____ **2.** One turkey was timed flying
  A. 5 feet per hour   **C.** 10 miles per hour
  B. 15 feet per hour   **D.** 55 miles per hour

_____ **3.** A turkey's snood can be found
  A. on its back   **C.** under the wing
  B. above the beak   **D.** above the eye

_____ **4.** A wattle is part of the turkey's
  A. neck   **C.** foot
  B. feathers   **D.** beak

_____ **5.** A turkey's wattle can turn from red to
  A. black   **C.** white
  B. blue   **D.** brown

Turkeys were once threatened birds. Wild turkeys lived in the woods. People cut down the woods to make roads, towns, and farms. The turkeys had no place to live. And people like to eat turkeys, so hunters killed many of these birds. By the 1900s the number of turkeys in America had dropped. Very few were left.

Leaders in each state knew that something had to be done. So they passed laws to solve the problem. Some laws placed limits on the number of turkeys that hunters could kill. Also, laws allowed some turkeys to be moved to areas where others had vanished. The new laws helped turkeys. And people learned that passing laws is one way to take care of wild animals.

_____ **6.** As people changed the land, wild turkeys
     A. flew straight up   **C.** lost their homes
     B. lived in towns   **D.** enjoyed people

_____ **7.** Hunters killed many turkeys for
     A. food   **C.** wattles
     B. beaks   **D.** feathers

_____ **8.** The turkeys were finally helped by
     A. experts   **C.** lawmakers
     B. hunters   **D.** soldiers

_____ **9.** Turkeys were saved by being moved to
     A. zoos   **C.** rolling hills
     B. other areas   **D.** cages

_____ **10.** The new laws
     A. helped hunters   **C.** were not passed
     B. did not work   **D.** saved the turkeys

Shivering Is Not Just Quivering

UNIT 17

Have you ever shivered on a cold day? You may not have noticed, but as you shivered, your body warmed up. Shivering is one way your body stays warm. It happens when signals are sent from the nervous system to the muscles. This is how it works.

The nervous system has two parts. One part is the nerves. They look like long, thin threads. Their job is to carry messages to all parts of the body. The spinal cord and the brain make up the other part of the nervous system. The spinal cord is a large bundle of nerves inside the backbone. Signals from the brain travel down the spinal cord. They go to the rest of the body through the nerves. Muscles receive these signals.

_____ **1.** Shivering helps your body
  A. keep calm   **C.** cool down
  B. stay warm   **D.** stand up straight

_____ **2.** Signals go from the nervous system to
  A. the muscles   **C.** the legs
  B. a certain cell   **D.** the nerves

_____ **3.** The nervous system has
  A. one part   **C.** two parts
  B. three parts   **D.** many parts

_____ **4.** Nerves look like
  A. muscles   **C.** blood cells
  B. threads   **D.** small trees

_____ **5.** The spinal cord is a large bundle of
  A. muscles   **C.** nerves
  B. brain cells **D.** signals

Steck-Vaughn • Comprehension Skills Series

Imagine waiting for a bus on a street corner. It's a cold day, the bus is late, and you feel chilled. Here's what happens.

A control center in your brain senses that you're cold. It sends a message down the spinal cord to all the nerves. The message races through nerves that connect to other nerves. Then it goes from the nerves to the muscles. The message says, "Warning! Prepare for action!"

When a muscle moves, it makes heat. That is why you get warm when you run or play soccer. When your muscles get the signal that you are cold, they get busy. First they become tight, then they loosen. They tighten then loosen over and over again. This makes you shiver. You also get warmer.

_____ **6.** Your brain's signal travels first to the
        A. bus   **C.** heart
        B. spinal cord   **D.** muscles

_____ **7.** Nerves tell the muscles to
        A. stop   **C.** get ready
        B. relax   **D.** cool down

_____ **8.** When a muscle moves, it becomes
        A. warm   **C.** stiff
        B. cool   **D.** heavy

_____ **9.** When you become cold, your muscles
        A. relax   **C.** stop moving
        B. stretch   **D.** tighten and loosen

_____ **10.** When you shiver, you get
        A. weaker   **C.** stronger
        B. colder   **D.** warmer

From Mowing Cloth to Mowing Grass

When people used to cut grass or grains in the fields, they used a tool called a scythe. It had a long handle and a curved, heavy blade. People swung the tool back and forth over and over again. It was backbreaking work.

Later, nobles and kings had lawns around their gardens. Some lawns stretched over large areas. But those who tended the lawns still used scythes to trim the grass.

At this time Edwin Budding worked in a cloth factory in England. When he went for walks outside his small town, he saw the gardeners hard at work. He wondered if there might be a better way to cut grass.

_____ **1.** A scythe has a
    A. motor   **C.** lawn
    B. button   **D.** blade

_____ **2.** People swung the heavy scythes
    A. up and down   **C.** over their heads
    B. in a circle   **D.** back and forth

_____ **3.** Some lawns of nobles were
    A. for sale   **C.** tiny
    B. large   **D.** under water

_____ **4.** Edwin Budding worked in a
    A. palace   **C.** cloth factory
    B. field   **D.** garden

_____ **5.** Edwin Budding saw the gardeners
    A. working   **C.** playing
    B. singing   **D.** eating

The cloth made at the factory where Budding worked was fuzzy. To trim the cloth, workers pushed it through two rollers. As the cloth passed between the rollers, blades passed over the cloth and trimmed the fuzz. Budding knew that the machine held the answer to the problem.

First Budding built a machine with long blades. Then he put the blades between two wheels. He placed a long handle on his new tool. Then he could push it without bending over.

In 1831 Budding's lawn mower was ready. But few people knew why such a machine might be useful. Most people didn't pay attention to it. But gardeners loved Budding's lawn mower. Today almost every house with a yard has one.

_____ **6.** Cloth made at the factory was
    A. cotton   **C.** fuzzy
    B. silk   **D.** brightly colored

_____ **7.** The cloth-trimming machine held
    A. problems   **C.** Budding's answer
    B. no help   **D.** wheels

_____ **8.** The long handle allowed Budding to
    A. go home   **C.** bend over
    B. trim cloth   **D.** stand up

_____ **9.** Budding's new machine was a
    A. cherry picker   **C.** washing machine
    B. lawn mower   **D.** cloth trimmer

_____ **10.** When gardeners saw the new tool, they
    A. laughed   **C.** loved it
    B. made cloth   **D.** quit their jobs

Bring More Water, Molly Pitcher

Molly Ludwig was a young girl when she met John Hays. She married him before she turned 15. They lived a quiet life in Pennsylvania. John worked as a barber, and Molly took care of their son.

Then their peaceful life changed. Many people felt that it was time for America to win its freedom from British rule. Along with his friends and neighbors, John joined the army.

Molly followed John into war. Like many young wives of the day, she washed and cooked for him while he fought in the war. She and John put up with the hardships of army life for three years.

_____ **1.** Molly married John before she was
   A. 19   **c.** 15
   B. 14   **D.** 20

_____ **2.** John worked as a
   A. lawyer   **c.** saddle maker
   B. doctor   **D.** barber

_____ **3.** Many people felt America should
   A. make laws   **c.** win its freedom
   B. make money   **D.** collect taxes

_____ **4.** John joined the
   A. British   **c.** local club
   B. army   **D.** barber school

_____ **5.** While John fought the war, Molly
   A. rode horses   **c.** laughed and played
   B. visited friends   **D.** washed and cooked

Molly was given a nickname by George Washington's troops. She hauled water to the men as they fought in battles. She carried the water in pitchers. One hot day as the men drank the cool water, they gave Molly her new name. They called her Molly Pitcher.

As she worked, Molly watched John fight. He was forcing cannonballs into a cannon with a long pole. All at once she saw him fall to the ground. She could tell he was hurt as he was moved off the field. Molly rushed to take his place at the cannon. She grabbed the pole and started to work. The battle went on as Molly fought in John's place. After the battle Molly joined the army. She served as a soldier for almost eight years.

_____ **6.** Molly earned her nickname by hauling
     A. water   **C.** cannons
     B. logs   **D.** meat

_____ **7.** Molly helped the soldiers during
     A. meals   **C.** illness
     B. marches   **D.** battles

_____ **8.** John put cannonballs in the cannon with
     A. a door   **C.** a pitcher
     B. water   **D.** a long pole

_____ **9.** When John fell, Molly took his
     A. pitcher   **C.** place
     B. horse   **D.** hat

_____ **10.** After the battle Molly became a
     A. teacher   **C.** nurse
     B. soldier   **D.** pilot

Sound Moves Air

The band played late into the night. The last song started with the loud beating of a drum. It ended with a harp played so softly that the people strained to hear it. They clapped and cheered when the song was over.

When people beat a drum or clap, the noise causes atoms in the air to move against each other. This movement makes a wave in the air. Sound waves travel through the air. They move the same way that a wave travels in water. Sound waves move from the source of the sound, through the air, to a person's ears. The outer part of the ear traps the sound waves. It sends them to the inner ear. There the waves of atoms push against the eardrums. Then the person hears sound.

_____ **1.** Noise causes atoms in the air to
   A. move   **C.** become wet
   B. clap   **D.** stop suddenly

_____ **2.** Sound waves travel through
   A. rocks   **C.** time
   B. air   **D.** dirt

_____ **3.** Sound waves travel like
   A. a bicycle   **C.** a speeding train
   B. the wind   **D.** waves in water

_____ **4.** The outer ear sends sound waves to the
   A. heart   **C.** inner ear
   B. skin   **D.** brain cells

_____ **5.** A person hears when atoms push against
   A. air   **C.** the outer ear
   B. water   **D.** the eardrums

Very soft sounds cause atoms to move slowly. But loud sounds send atoms into wild motion. Sound waves caused by loud sounds can hurt a person's eardrums.

Years ago experts measured the speed of sound waves. They found that sound waves travel at a speed of 750 miles per hour. This speed is the same for loud sounds and for soft sounds.

Today some airplanes can travel faster than 750 miles per hour. When this happens, people for miles around hear a loud boom. This noise is called a sonic boom. It happens when the atoms in a sound wave push against each other.

_____ **6.** Very soft sounds cause atoms to
    A. stop   **C.** move wildly
    B. boom   **D.** move gently

_____ **7.** Very loud sounds can cause eardrums to
    A. dance   **C.** be hurt
    B. relax   **D.** get better

_____ **8.** Sound waves travel at the speed of
    A. airplanes   **C.** 750 miles per hour
    B. light   **D.** 570 miles per hour

_____ **9.** If a plane travels very fast, people will
    A. hear a boom   **C.** watch the plane
    B. take cover   **D.** "see" sound

_____ **10.** A sonic boom happens when atoms
    A. split   **C.** come together
    B. roll   **D.** move apart

Made for the Job

If you looked at a bald eagle, it would stare back at you. But the eagle would see you more clearly than you see it. Birds can see better than other animals. And eagles can see better than other birds. An eagle can see three to eight times better than a human can. This helps it with its main job, hunting. While an eagle glides high in the air, it can spot a fish in a stream far below.

An eagle must fly great distances in search of food. Its wings also help it hunt. When an eagle's wings are spread out, they stretch out six or seven feet. These large wings can carry an eagle over a hundred miles in a day.

_____ **1.** If you looked at a bald eagle, it would
    A. squawk   **C.** fly away
    B. blink   **D.** stare back

_____ **2.** An eagle's sharp eyes help it
    A. sleep   **C.** find a mate
    B. hunt   **D.** fly

_____ **3.** While it is flying, an eagle looks for
    A. food   **C.** feathers
    B. humans   **D.** other eagles

_____ **4.** An eagle's wings can measure
    A. three feet   **C.** fifteen feet
    B. five feet   **D.** seven feet

_____ **5.** In a day an eagle can fly more than
    A. 600 miles   **C.** 100 miles
    B. 700 miles   **D.** 1,000 miles

When a hungry eagle sees a fish, it swoops down at top speed toward the stream. Then it snatches the fish with its sharp claws. These claws are called talons. The talons are at least one inch long. They grasp the fish tightly as the eagle soars upward. The toes and the bottoms of the eagle's feet are covered with hundreds of tiny bumps. These bumps help it hold the slippery fish.

The eagle might carry the fish to shore. There the eagle's pointed beak helps it eat the fish. An eagle uses its beak to catch prey and to tear meat.

_____ **6.** When a hungry eagle sees a fish, it
  A. calls out   **C.** flies higher
  B. dives   **D.** flies away

_____ **7.** An eagle picks up its food with its
  A. feet   **C.** eyes
  B. wings   **D.** feathers

_____ **8.** An eagle's talons
  A. help it see   **C.** help it fly
  B. are not sharp   **D.** catch its food

_____ **9.** The tiny bumps on an eagle's feet help it
  A. fly   **C.** hold its food
  B. see   **D.** soar upward

_____ **10.** An eagle's pointed beak helps it to
  A. fly   **C.** crack seeds
  B. eat   **D.** grab branches

Good Night, Don't Bite!

There's nothing quite like falling sound asleep after a full day of work. Like people, animals need to rest after working hard. Some animals sleep floating in water. Others dig holes under the ground. Some even sleep high in trees or under leaves. But they all find a way to rest.

Animals sleeping in the sea can be a strange sight. Fish sleep with their eyes open. They do not have eyelids, so they seem to stare into the depths while they nap. Sea otters sometimes sleep in beds of seaweed. This keeps them from floating away. Parrotfish blow a clear gel from their mouths when they are ready to snooze. The gel forms a bubble around them. The bubble protects them from harm while they sleep.

_____ **1.** Like people, animals need to
- **A.** cry
- **B.** talk
- **C.** rest
- **D.** tell time

_____ **2.** Fish do not have
- **A.** scales
- **B.** bubbles
- **C.** tails
- **D.** eyelids

_____ **3.** Sea otters sometimes sleep in
- **A.** holes
- **B.** seaweed
- **C.** boats
- **D.** caves

_____ **4.** Parrotfish make a clear gel with their
- **A.** mouths
- **B.** scales
- **C.** skin
- **D.** fins

_____ **5.** Parrotfish sleep in a bubble that
- **A.** shrinks
- **B.** glows
- **C.** grows large
- **D.** protects them

Steck-Vaughn • Comprehension Skills Series

Other animals sleep under the ground. Chipmunks sleep curled up in a ball. Their beds are made of leaves and grass. They wake up now and then to snack on food stored nearby. Some desert frogs dig underground holes during the hot, dry season. A frog may stay in its hole for months.

High above the ground, monkeys make leafy nests in trees each evening before they retire. The tree's high branches help to keep the monkeys safe during the night. Even the insects buzzing around their heads rest. Some sleep under a leaf that will be their next meal. A bee might crawl down into a blossom to rest. When it crawls out the next morning, it is rested and ready to buzz off to work.

_____ **6.** Chipmunks sleep in beds made of
    A. nets   **C.** leaves and grass
    B. mud   **D.** sticks and twigs

_____ **7.** Desert frogs stay underground during
    A. morning   **C.** the night
    B. winter   **D.** the hot, dry season

_____ **8.** Monkeys make beds using material from
    A. insects   **C.** the ground
    B. water   **D.** trees

_____ **9.** Some insects rest
    A. while eating   **C.** while buzzing
    B. under leaves   **D.** curled up in a ball

_____**10.** A bee might sleep in
    A. a flower   **C.** a bubble
    B. mud   **D.** clear gel

Stop That Pacing, Fido!

If you are planning a picnic, watch your pets. If your dog paces and your cat twitches, make other plans. It may rain that day. Or if you want to wash your car, go outside early in the day and look for a spider. If you see a spider spinning a web, get out your soap and bucket. There will most likely be fair weather.

If you would rather fly a kite, look at the stars the night before. If they are bright, find your kite and string. It will be windy the next day. But if you are more in the mood for a swim, listen to the crickets. By counting their chirps, you can tell if it is warm enough.

_____ **1.** If your cat twitches as you plan a picnic,
   A. wash your car   **C.** take more food
   B. go swimming   **D.** make other plans

_____ **2.** A spider spinning a web means
   A. rain   **C.** fair weather
   B. clouds   **D.** snow

_____ **3.** If you want to fly a kite, look at the
   A. dust   **C.** grass
   B. crickets   **D.** stars

_____ **4.** If you want to swim, listen to the
   A. crickets   **C.** cats
   B. dogs   **D.** spiders

_____ **5.** To tell about weather, count a cricket's
   A. legs   **C.** eyes
   B. chirps   **D.** wings

What do animals know about weather? Dampness collects in the air before a rain. It makes each hair in an animal's fur swell. That is why your pets move about restlessly. Spiders do not like dampness in the air, either. A spider web will not stick to a damp surface. So if a spider is spinning a web, the air must be dry.

How can stars help you plan your fun? Stars are most easily seen when winds high in the air blow dust and clouds away. These winds will drop to the ground the next day, making it windy. And what about those crickets? Count the number of times a cricket chirps in 15 seconds. Then add 37 to find out how warm it is. So if you hear 35 chirps, it is 72 degrees.

_____ **6.** Dampness in the air makes an animal
  A. hungry   **C.** restless
  B. warm   **D.** smaller

_____ **7.** If a spider is spinning, the air must be
  A. damp   **C.** dry
  B. fresh   **D.** hot

_____ **8.** Strong winds high in the air blow away
  A. fur   **C.** stars
  B. webs   **D.** clouds

_____ **9.** If you see bright stars, there will be wind
  A. in a month **C.** the following day
  B. in a week   **D.** in two days

_____**10.** A cricket's chirps can help tell if it's
  A. warm   **C.** cloudy
  B. rainy   **D.** dusk

Cooking Trees

You may know that the paper in this book came from trees. But did you know that parts of the trees were cooked to make the paper? Trees are cut into chips when they are first brought from the woods. The chips are piled like giant sand dunes around paper mills. These chips are cooked at the paper mills to make paper.

Strong fibers in the chips become paper. A glue called lignin holds the fibers together. The chips are placed in cookers as big as round swimming pools. There special powders take out the lignin, and the chips become pulp. The pulp looks like cooked, white oatmeal. After it is cleaned, the pulp is poured into a beater. The beater is like a huge home mixer. It whips the pulp until it is as smooth as a fine cake batter.

_____ 1. Piles of wood chips look like
   A. sand dunes   **C.** a mixer
   B. powders   **D.** oatmeal

_____ 2. To make paper, wood chips are put in a
   A. hole   **C.** cooker
   B. liquid   **D.** glue

_____ 3. The wood fibers are held together by a
   A. pulp   **C.** batter
   B. glue   **D.** chip

_____ 4. Special powders remove the
   A. fibers   **C.** lignin
   B. trees   **D.** juice

_____ 5. The pulp is whipped until it is
   A. white   **C.** powder
   B. smooth   **D.** lumpy

Pumps spray the pulp onto a large moving screen. Most of the water drains through the screen. A mat of wood fibers is left behind. Large rollers squeeze the rest of the water from the mat.

The mat is pressed into a solid sheet. Then it is dried as it goes through heated rollers. At this stage the pulp has become paper. When the paper leaves the heated rollers, it is wrapped onto rolls as tall as a building.

The giant rolls are shipped to other factories to be made into paper products. After it is cut, the paper might become napkins, tissue paper, notebook paper, or a book such as the one you are reading.

_____ **6.** When the pulp is on the screen, the water
      A. cooks   **C.** evaporates
      B. drains   **D.** turns to glue

_____ **7.** Next the fibers are pressed into a solid
      A. layer   **C.** square
      B. rock   **D.** ball

_____ **8.** The mat is dried by
      A. pumps   **C.** strong fibers
      B. cookers   **D.** heated rollers

_____ **9.** After the paper is dried, it is put
      A. in piles   **C.** onto enormous rolls
      B. on a train   **D.** into the cooker

_____ **10.** At factories the paper might be made into
      A. plastic   **C.** tissue paper
      B. batter   **D.** glue

Louis Braille

Louis Braille was born in a small French town. When he was three, he lost his sight. At ten he went to a school for children who were blind. The books at his school were written with raised letters. He moved his fingers over the letters to read the books. But letters like *A* and *H* felt the same. He had a hard time understanding what he read.

Then Louis learned of a different way to read. It was used by soldiers who had to read messages in the dark. To write the messages, people punched dots in paper. Since the dots were raised, people could feel them.

_____ **1.** Louis Braille was born in
    A. Spain   **C.** England
    B. France   **D.** the United States

_____ **2.** Louis lost his sight when he was
    A. two   **C.** ten
    B. three   **D.** fifteen

_____ **3.** To read books Louis used
    A. his fingers   **C.** a machine
    B. his eyes   **D.** his mother's help

_____ **4.** Louis had a hard time understanding
    A. his friends   **C.** what he heard
    B. his teachers **D.** what he read

_____ **5.** The system with raised dots was used by
    A. miners   **C.** doctors
    B. soldiers   **D.** forest rangers

Louis liked the idea of reading with raised dots. But he thought it could be made simpler. So when Louis was fifteen, he made up a new way of writing. He used raised dots, but he made up his own alphabet.

All of Louis's friends at school liked his idea. But many teachers did not want to use it. They thought the old way worked just fine. Then in 1844 this new way of reading and writing was shown to the public. When more people saw how it worked, they liked it. Today people all over the world read books written in Braille.

_____ **6.** Louis decided to use the idea of reading
      A. old books   **C.** raised dots
      B. aloud   **D.** picture books

_____ **7.** Louis's new system used
      A. small letters   **C.** no raised dots
      B. a machine   **D.** a new alphabet

_____ **8.** Louis's friends thought his system
      A. was strange   **C.** worked well
      B. was too hard   **D.** did not work

_____ **9.** At first the new system was not used by
      A. parents   **C.** the government
      B. students   **D.** people who taught school

_____ **10.** Today Braille's system
      A. is not used   **C.** does not work
      B. is well liked   **D.** is used only in France

Writing

Read the story below. Think about the facts. Then answer the questions in complete sentences.

Mount Everest is the tallest mountain in the world. It rises five-and-a-half miles above sea level. This great peak lies north of India between Nepal and Tibet.

Many climbers have tried to scale Mount Everest. Some have made it to the top. The climb is hard for many reasons. The air is thin and cold at that height. Winds are strong. There are cracks in the snow and ice where climbers might fall.

In 1953 two men became the first to reach the top. They were Sir Edmund Hillary and Tenzing Norgay. The climb took more than two months.

1. How tall is Mount Everest?

_____

_____

2. Where is Mount Everest located?

_____

_____

3. Who reached the top of Mount Everest first?

_____

_____

To check your answers, turn to page 60.

Prewriting

Think of an idea you might write about, such as a well-known place or person. Write the idea in the center of the idea web below. Then fill out the rest of the web with facts.

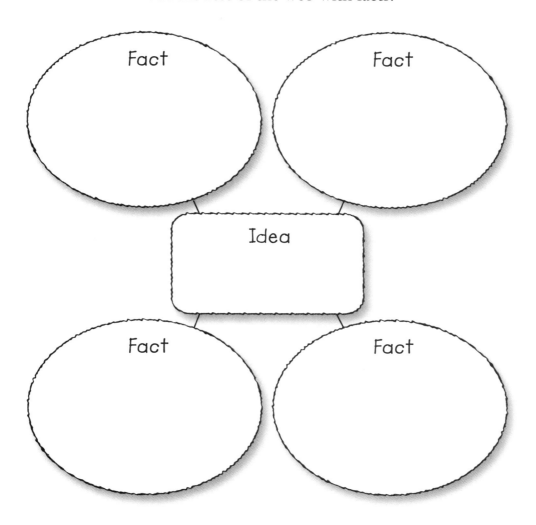

On Your Own

Now use another sheet of paper to write a story about your idea. Use the facts from your idea web.

To check your answers, turn to page 60.

Check Yourself

What Are Facts? Page 2

Fact: Opals are stones that sparkle with many colors.
Fact: Coober Pedy is in South Australia.

Practice Finding Facts, Page 3

3. D

To check your answers to pages 6–29, see page 61.

Writing, Page 30

Possible answers include:

1. A comet looks like a fuzzy star with a tail.
2. The tail looks long and bright when the comet flies near the sun.
3. Halley's Comet can be seen about every 77 years.

Writing, Page 31

Check that you have four facts in your story.

To check your answers to pages 32–57, see page 62.

Writing, Page 58

Possible answers include:

1. Mount Everest is five-and-a-half miles above sea level.
2. Mount Everest is north of India between Nepal and Tibet.
3. Sir Edmund Hillary and Tenzing Norgay reached the top of Mount Everest first.

Writing, Page 59

Check that you have four facts in your story.

Steck-Vaughn • Comprehension Skills Series

Check Yourself

Unit 1 pp. 6–7	Unit 2 pp. 8–9	Unit 3 pp. 10–11	Unit 4 pp. 12–13	Unit 5 pp. 14–15	Unit 6 pp. 16–17	Unit 7 pp. 18–19	Unit 8 pp. 20–21	Unit 9 pp. 22–23	Unit 10 pp. 24–25	Unit 11 pp. 26–27	Unit 12 pp. 28–29
1. D	1. D	1. C	1. B	1. C	1. B	1. B	1. C	1. A	1. A	1. C	1. A
2. B	2. D	2. D	2. C	2. B	2. B	2. C	2. B	2. A	2. C	2. C	2. D
3. C	3. A	3. D	3. C	3. C	3. A	3. D	3. B	3. C	3. C	3. A	3. A
4. D	4. C	4. C	4. C	4. D	4. C	4. D	4. D	4. D	4. D	4. B	4. C
5. B	5. B	5. D	5. B	5. B	5. D	5. B	5. C	5. D	5. C	5. C	5. C
6. C	6. C	6. A	6. B	6. D	6. B	6. C	6. A	6. A	6. A	6. B	6. D
7. A	7. D	7. C	7. D	7. D	7. C	7. A	7. A	7. D	7. B	7. A	7. B
8. C	8. A	8. B	8. D	8. D	8. D	8. D	8. C	8. C	8. D	8. A	8. C
9. A	9. D	9. D	9. C	9. B	9. A	9. C	9. B	9. B	9. D	9. D	9. C
10. C	10. B	10. A	10. A	10. D	10. D	10. A	10. C	10. D	10. C	10. D	10. A

Unit 13 pp. 32–33	Unit 14 pp. 34–35	Unit 15 pp. 36–37	Unit 16 pp. 38–39	Unit 17 pp. 40–41	Unit 18 pp. 42–43	Unit 19 pp. 44–45	Unit 20 pp. 46–47	Unit 21 pp. 48–49	Unit 22 pp. 50–51	Unit 23 pp. 52–53	Unit 24 pp. 54–55	Unit 25 pp. 56–57
1. C	1. C	1. C	1. C	1. B	1. D	1. C	1. A	1. D	1. C	1. D	1. A	1. B
2. A	2. C	2. C	2. D	2. A	2. D	2. D	2. B	2. B	2. D	2. C	2. C	2. B
3. B	3. D	3. B	3. B	3. C	3. B	3. C	3. D	3. A	3. B	3. D	3. B	3. A
4. A	4. A	4. D	4. A	4. B	4. C	4. B	4. C	4. D	4. A	4. A	4. C	4. D
5. D	5. B	5. D	5. C	5. C	5. A	5. D	5. D	5. C	5. D	5. B	5. B	5. B
6. C	6. D	6. C	6. C	6. B	6. C	6. A	6. D	6. B	6. C	6. C	6. B	6. C
7. D	7. B	7. C	7. A	7. C	7. C	7. D	7. C	7. A	7. D	7. C	7. A	7. D
8. C	8. B	8. B	8. C	8. A	8. D	8. D	8. C	8. D	8. D	8. D	8. D	8. C
9. D	9. A	9. A	9. B	9. D	9. B	9. C	9. A	9. C	9. B	9. C	9. C	9. D
10. A	10. D	10. D	10. D	10. D	10. C	10. B	10. C	10. B	10. A	10. A	10. C	10. B